# CHRISTIANITY AND THE ROLE OF PHILOSOPHY

# CHRISTIANITY AND THE ROLE OF PHILOSOPHY

## K. SCOTT OLIPHINT

PHILADELPHIA, PENNSYLVANIA

**P&R PUBLISHING**

P.O. BOX 817 • PHILLIPSBURG • NEW JERSEY 08865-0817

Westminster Seminary Press, LLC, a Pennsylvania Limited Liability Company, is a wholly owned subsidiary of Westminster Theological Seminary.

This work is a co-publication between P&R Publishing and Westminster Seminary Press, LLC.

Scripture quotations are from *ESV Bible* ® (*The Holy Bible, English Standard Version* ®). Copyright © 2001 by Crossway Bibles, a publishing ministry of Good News Publishers. Used by permission. All rights reserved.

Italics within Scripture quotations indicate emphasis added.

ISBN: 978-1-59638-674-7

Printed in the United States of America

Library of Congress Control Number: 2013939997

*Wisdom is a most beautiful thing, and love is of the beautiful; and therefore love is also a philosopher or lover of wisdom. (Plato, Symposium, 204b)*

*Where is the one who is wise? Where is the scribe? Where is the debater of this age? Has not God made foolish the wisdom of the world? (1 Cor. 1:20)*

## INTRODUCTION

The word *philosophy* means "love of wisdom." Historically, philosophy has been characterized by a relentless search for wisdom, a single-minded and insatiable desire to set forth the fundamental aspects of human existence in order to guide human activity. In the words of the pre-Socratic philosopher Heraclitus, "Wisdom is to speak the truth and act in keeping with its nature." Philosophy is concerned with the truth and with actions that are in accordance with the way things are. This requires some notion of just what "truth" is, and it requires that we know something of "the way things are."

So what exactly is philosophy? Generally speaking, it is a theoretical activity that seeks to make sense out of the world in order to make sense of our place in it. In its activity, historically, philosophy has concerned itself with three broad categories: *metaphysics, epistemology,* and *ethics.*

*Metaphysics* asks and attempts to answer the question: "What is the nature of things in reality, and especially of *ultimate* reality?"

In asking these kinds of questions, metaphysics seeks to get to the "essence" of a thing, or to define it in a way that promotes a deeper understanding of it.

The term itself was likely first used around 70 B.C. and attributed to some of Aristotle's works. Aristotle wrote *Physica* to deal with the things that were physical or substantial, things that pertained primarily to the senses. But he also wrote a section that he called at times "First Philosophy," sometimes "Wisdom," and even at times "Theology." One of his followers entitled the work *Metaphysica*, which means "that which is beside or over or above the physical." Metaphysics, then, deals with that which is above and beyond the physical, that which is ultimate and real.

*Epistemology* is a term that came into philosophical vocabulary much later. It first appeared in German in the latter part of the eighteenth century as *Erkentnisstheorie* and then later came into English as *epistemology*. It is taken from the Greek word *episteme* and means "study of knowledge." Philosophy's task here is to study why, how, or *whether* we know something. Aristotle began his work on metaphysics with this statement: "All men by nature desire to know." Here we see the interweaving of metaphysics and epistemology. Aristotle is saying something about the *nature* of man, which would have something to do with metaphysics. He is also asserting that it is a part of man's nature to want to *know*, which touches on the area of epistemology. This discussion of epistemology together with metaphysics was typical of philosophy for most of its history.

Since the Enlightenment, however, the two disciplines have, for the most part, been separated, and metaphysics has been all but ignored. Though the discipline of metaphysics is currently making a comeback, epistemology took over the field of interest in philosophy at the time of Immanuel Kant (late eighteenth century).

*Ethics*—sometimes called *moral philosophy*—concerns itself with either of two primary categories. It may concern itself with so-called judgments of value, in which philosophers look at judgments of approval/disapproval, rightness/wrongness of an action, and so on. Or it may focus on so-called judgments of obligation, in which philosophers attempt to determine what it is we are obligated to do or not obligated to do in given situations or circumstances.

These three categories have constituted the bulk of philosophical activity since its inception.

Our particular interest here, however, is the *role* of philosophy. More specifically, our interest is to argue for the proper *place* of philosophy as a theoretical discipline. How might we go about such an argument? There are likely a number of ways to attempt to put philosophy in its proper place and thus to determine its proper role. Our path of choice will be to focus on the *subject matter* of philosophy in order to clarify its place and its role.

As we saw above, philosophy's subject matter is normally seen to be the three (broad) areas of metaphysics, epistemology, and ethics. Thus, it sets itself the tasks of asking broad and basic questions about reality: What is the nature of a thing or of reality itself? How can we know anything, and what is that knowledge? What is the right (or wrong) action to take in this particular circumstance, or in the world?

### Before we move on

+ What is the chief task of philosophy?
+ What questions do metaphysics, epistemology, and ethics each seek to answer?
+ Given its concern with these issues, how is philosophy relevant to daily life?

## "KNOW THYSELF"

A significant, perhaps predominant, part of philosophical discussion has been concerned with knowing, and with knowing the nature of things. The natural place to start with such concerns is with yourself. In knowing yourself, you know something about your *nature*, so metaphysics is a part of this knowledge. In knowing yourself, you know something about *knowing*, so epistemology is included. In knowing yourself, you would know "virtue," as Socrates himself argued, so ethics is implied as well.

So Socrates, borrowing a phrase from the Oracle of Delphi, summarized his own approach to philosophy with the pithy command "Know Thyself." Presumably, we can obtain knowledge of ourselves and this knowledge will have something to do with our knowledge of the world as well. To know yourself truly includes not simply that you are a human being, or that you are six feet tall, but also that you are Socrates and not Plato, that you reside in Athens, not in Sparta, and so forth.

In pursuit of self-knowledge, philosophy began to ask questions about what is good and what is not. This question was not only an ethical question; it was much more than that. It was, at root, a metaphysical question. It was a question that led one to begin to think about what might be the highest good (*summum bonum*) and how we might know it. For Plato, the highest good was Goodness itself, and good things here on Earth were partial examples of this Goodness. Those things that I do that are good, therefore, are good only because they have their reference point in the highest Goodness. Or, to put it another way, the good things that you do and the good things that I do are not simply different "goodnesses." If that were the case, there would be no relationship between your good and my good. In order for them to be properly related, they must be examples of the one true Goodness.

8

While the command to "Know Thyself" might initially appear simple enough, it becomes more complicated when combined with a commitment to the "love of wisdom" (philosophy).

B E F O R E  W E  M O V E  O N

✦ Why is self-knowledge the obvious starting point for philosophy, and how does it relate to the three broad categories of philosophy?

✦ How do questions about goodness also relate to metaphysics, epistemology, and ethics?

## ARE WE THERE YET?

From its earliest days to the present, philosophy has been pursuing Socrates's mandate, "Know Thyself." This pursuit has generated an enormous amount of discussion, argument, debate, and dialogue. The different topics of philosophy—metaphysics, epistemology, and ethics—have taken on lives of their own such that, in many cases, the question of self-knowledge is barely visible. In the end, however, that question still lies near the center of philosophy's concern.

So after a few thousand years, how has philosophy done? Where are we now, given that some of the best and brightest minds have set themselves the task of knowing the nature of themselves and the world? Unfortunately, at least by some estimates, progress has been all too slow.

For example, one modern philosopher has boldly declared that even into the twenty-first century, after over four thousand years of discussion, no one metaphysical theory has won the philosophical day. He contrasts metaphysical theories with the body of knowledge currently available in geology, to use just one example, and notes:

9

In the end we must confess that we have no idea why there is no established body of metaphysical results. It cannot be denied that this is a fact, however, and the beginning student of metaphysics should keep this fact and its implications in mind. One of its implications is that the author of this book ... is [not] in a position in relation to you that is like the position of the author of [a] text ... in geology .... All of these people will be the masters of a certain body of knowledge, and, on many matters, if you disagree with them you will simply be wrong. In metaphysics, however, you are perfectly free to disagree with anything the acknowledged experts say—other than their assertions about what philosophers have said in the past or are saying at present.[1]

This is a stunning assertion. Even if some philosophers would quarrel with it, it cannot be denied that many would agree with this analysis. Not only so, but an argument could be made (though it won't be made here) that what goes for metaphysics goes also for epistemology and ethics. There seems to have been far too little, perhaps even no, progress on the three big questions that philosophers have perennially asked. The quest to "Know Thyself" remains in almost total darkness. There seems to be no philosophical consensus on who we are, on what the world is like, on how we might know, or might know that we know, and on what is right and what is wrong. Would another four thousand years give us a consensus? Do we simply need more time for philosophical speculation? What's a lover of wisdom to do?

### Before we move on

+ After thousands of years of consideration, why might philosophers have failed to establish an agreed-on metaphysical theory?

## A GPS OR A ROAD MAP?

Whenever we decide to go somewhere, the most crucial thing to know, first of all, is not where we're going, but where we *are*. We cannot know which way we are supposed to be going until and unless we know where we are.

Let's propose two different ways to try to figure out where we are (in order, eventually, to know where we're going). The first way is a road map. Suppose we are in a strange place, but we have a fairly detailed road map that we are using to try to figure out how to get to our destination. The first thing we have to do is to know where we actually are. Perhaps how we got to where we are now is a bit of a mystery; maybe we seem to have simply "appeared" someplace. So we look around and notice that we are at the corner of Elm and Twenty-first Street. We look at the map, and lo and behold, there is the intersection of Elm and Twenty-first Street. We hope, therefore, to trace out a route and proceed along on our map, road by road, until we see our destination.

But it just so happens that we cannot find our destination, no matter how many roads we trace from Elm and Twenty-first Street. The problem, it seems, is that the intersection of Elm and Twenty-first Street on the map must be a different intersection from where we are. Maybe we're in a different state from the one traced on our road map, or a different county or township from the one pictured on our map. What we need is another map, a map of the correct state, county, or township. Once that map is secured, we can then locate the intersection of Elm and Twenty-first Street. But how will we go about finding the correct state, county, or township? Could it be that there are a number of intersections of Elm and Twenty-first Street in a number of states and counties? This could take some time. The best that we'll be able to do is to try different road maps in hopes of finding in at least one of them where we actually are.

The problem with this method of determination is that we really do not know *where* we are. We have some idea of our surroundings, but to locate those surroundings in such a way that they conform to the map requires much more knowledge than we currently have. Not only so, but this method of discovery begins with ourselves and our own limited abilities. All we have to go on in seeking our location and destination is what little we know of what is around us. Attempting to move out with such scant knowledge in order to find our desired destination will virtually guarantee that we will never get where we want to go.

Using the scenario above, the second way to find out where we are is to use a global positioning system (GPS). We turn on the GPS, and within a few seconds the map is given on the screen, showing us exactly where we are. All that is left for us to do is to punch in our destination. Once we do that, we are shown how to get there, and how long it will take before we arrive.

Philosophy, by and large, in its quest for and love of wisdom, has tied itself to the first way above. It has sought to discover the answer to its three big questions by looking around its limited surroundings, using whatever maps may be available at the time, and moving inexorably toward some destination. As we saw above, however, there has been little to no progress. As the first way illustrates, this is the case because not only has philosophy remained ignorant of its own "location," it has determined to assess that "location," as well as its destination, beginning from whatever map is currently available. But just what that map is, or whether it can help us in our current quandary, is anybody's guess. The best we can do is to keep employing different maps, hoping that, perchance, we might find where we are and thus get to our desired goal.

The first way has proved to be a failure; it has not allowed philosophy to move off its initial mark. It may continue to hold out hope that the right road map will one day appear. Until then, it will pick and choose road maps, in hopes that one will provide a way forward. But this will not do. What philosophy needs, and has needed all along, is a GPS. Its only hope for real progress is in adopting the second way.

BEFORE WE MOVE ON

✠ What are the problems with the map method described?

✠ How does a GPS overcome those problems?

✠ What methods have many philosophers used to answer philosophy's big questions?

## THE VIEW FROM ABOVE

It will not escape the alert reader that the three big areas that we have laid out as central to philosophy are also central areas of discussion in the Christian faith. It may be the case that the questions are phrased differently. It may be that most Christians would not ask, "What is the nature of ultimate reality?" or "How do I know *that*?" Even so, fundamental to Christianity is a response to both of those key questions.

But there is a crucial difference in the Christian response to those questions. The response comes, first and foremost, not from Christians, but from God himself. In terms of our illustration above, Christians are not left with a road map that may or may not help with their current location. Christians have been given a view from above. They have a "GPS" that comes down from above to explain to them where they are and how they can get to where they need to go.

This "GPS" is God's revelation in all its forms. It includes God's revelation in creation, his revelation in his Word, and preeminently his revelation in the Lord Jesus Christ. Apart from God's declaring himself and his will to us, we could not know how to please him, nor could we know what he is like. But because we have this revelation, we can begin to get to the truth of the matter with respect to the three big questions that philosophy has pursued these millennia.

So the answer to the metaphysical question that philosophy asks, "What is the nature of ultimate reality?" is "The triune God." And his existence as the one God includes the three persons, each of whom is fully and completely this one God. Christianity understands that there is nothing more ultimate than God, and that he alone exists by virtue of who he is. He does not exist because of something else. He simply *is*. The only reason that we *are* is that he has given us existence.[2]

Likewise, the initial answer to the epistemological question "How do I know?" is: "God has spoken." Since God alone has the "view from above," and since he has spoken in his Word and in his world, that which he communicates is true knowledge. When God says, "In the beginning, God created the heavens and the earth" (Gen. 1:1), it is the case that God created all things, and that before creation there was nothing but the triune God. In the same way that we can know where we are and where we should go because the GPS view from above shows us, so also we know who we are and what we are to do and be because God speaks to us.

More obviously, perhaps, what is right and what is wrong is precisely what God says is right and wrong. As God has revealed himself in various ways and at various times in history, he has made known just what is required to please him during those times. He has also made known what he requires of us, his creatures, throughout history. He has revealed himself climactically in his Son, the Lord Jesus Christ; and since Christ has come, he has revealed in his spoken Word, the Bible, just what our responsibilities are to him. The ethical questions have their answers in what God has said in his Word.

BEFORE WE MOVE ON

✤ What makes the Christian response to philosophical questions different from other responses?

✤ How can Christians answer the specific questions of metaphysics, epistemology, and ethics?

## AT THE INTERSECTION

Given the intersection of the concerns of Christian theology with the questions of philosophy, one can construe the relationship between the two in at least four ways.

1. Philosophy "governs" theology. This view holds that because philosophy deals with the totality of reality, part of its task is to delineate the boundaries and activities of every other discipline. An example of one holding this view is Herman Dooyeweerd.[3] According to Dooyeweerd, philosophy assigns to theology its place and its task. That is what is meant by *govern*.

2. Philosophy is to be integrated with theology. This view is more ambiguous than 1, since the notion of *integration* is not always clear. Does philosophy "integrate" with theology when theology uses philosophical vocabulary? Historically, the answer to this question has been no. But the notion of *integration* in this category should be seen as on a continuum; it can be "more or less." In terms of his method of doing philosophy, Thomas Aquinas argued that the knowledge of God could be had by using certain tools of philosophy. This knowledge of God could be acquired by reason alone. This is most likely the majority view in the history of the church and of Christians doing philosophy.

Such a view depends on a particular view of the relationship of natural theology to special revelation. Natural theology is something that anyone can do as long as the right tools of reason are employed. Special revelation, though, is also necessary to fill out or supplement the proper conclusions of natural theology.

3. Philosophy is theology. The *is* here is not *is* in terms of identity but rather in terms of subject matter. This view can be seen, for example, in John Scotus Erigena in the Middle Ages, in some forms of Deism, and in certain forms of modern theology (e.g., Paul Tillich's "ground of being"). The main tenet of this position is that the way to God is through reason alone. Revelation either is not appealed to or is denied altogether as an authority, as in Tillich. The subject matter discussed deals very little with biblical revelation and almost exclusively with abstract ideas or systems of thought.

4. Theology "governs" philosophy. This is the Reformed view of the two disciplines, and is the view that we will now attempt to explain and develop.

BEFORE WE MOVE ON

+ In one view, philosophy governs theology. In another, theology governs philosophy. What might "governing" look like in either view?

+ In order to integrate philosophy with theology, what must be believed regarding natural revelation?

+ The view that philosophy *is* theology leads to what position on biblical revelation? Why?

## GROUNDING AND FOUNDING

Now that we have outlined some of the issues involved, just how do we go about understanding the relationship of philosophy to theology? One way to go about it would be to set out the general subject matter of each discipline. This is a necessary first step, in that we need to know just what the content of each discipline is. The subject matter of theology and of philosophy will help us understand what place each should have with respect to the other.

But there is another, more foundational aspect to each of these disciplines that is crucial to defining their respective place and role. Simply to note the subject matter of each discipline, while important, is not sufficient for our purposes. We must also consider the foundation of philosophy and theology. Historically, the foundation of a discipline was termed its *principium*. This Latin word looks much like our English word *principle*. If we take the basic dictionary definition of *principle* as "that which is the foundation of a given system or discipline," we can begin to see its importance. But *principium* means more than simply a principle. It also includes the idea of a *source* and *ground* of a particular discipline. *Principia*, therefore, are those basic, fundamental, and necessary truths that provide for the existence and coherence of a particular discipline.

So it should help us to think of theology and philosophy in terms of the historical notion of *principia*. Under this rubric, distinctions have been made between a *principium essendi* (which is a principle, source, or ground of the existence of something) and a *principium cognoscendi* (which is a principle, source, or ground of the knowledge of something). There are, then, two central *principia*: that which is for existence, an essential foundation and source; and that which is for knowledge, an epistemological foundation and source.[4]

Before we move on

+ What is the difference between a foundation and a source? How are these two concepts both present in the word *principium*?

✢ What is the difference between a *principium essendi* and a *principium cognoscendi*? How might these relate to the concerns of philosophy?

Now the question of the differences between philosophy and theology will revolve around the answers to the questions of philosophy's and theology's *principia*. What is philosophy's *principium cognoscendi* (principle of knowledge)? That, of course, depends on whom you ask. For the most part, however, it has been assumed that philosophy's *principium cognoscendi* is reason itself. Without reason's asking and answering of questions, there could be no philosophy at all.

To answer the question of *principia* is to answer, as well, the question of authority. The reason, cause, or source of a discipline, in this sense, gives it its justification; it points to its boundaries and its rules or laws. If reason is the *principium cognoscendi* of philosophy, then philosophy's boundaries are determined by reason, its authority lies in reason, and its rules and laws are the rules and laws of reason. Not only so, but suppose we ask what the *principium essendi* of philosophy is. What gives it its existence, its ground, its foundation? Here again, the answer would likely be "reason." It seems, then, that with respect to philosophy, the *principium essendi* (essential principle) has been made identical to the *principium cognoscendi*. But this has the potential of creating some serious problems.

The first problem lies in the area of authority. If we suppose that reason is the *principium cognoscendi* of philosophy, then that would include the notion that philosophy's authority is as strong, say, as the laws of logic, or the force of a sound argument, or something like that. In that way, one accepts philosophy's conclusions as one accepts these laws and forces. But nagging questions still remain. Where did these laws come from, and what kind of laws are they? Are they eternal, unchangeable laws? Conventions of society? So intuitive that no one can disagree and thus consent-compelling?

In theology, the *principia* are clearly laid out. The standard view in theology is that its *principium essendi* is God himself. He is the source of our understanding of himself, and of all other things. He creates them, sustains them, directs them according to his eternal counsel, and guides them for the sake of his own glory. He is the source, the foundation, the ground, and the justification of theology (and of all else). Not only so, but he alone provides what is needed for us to understand him and his revelation to us. The *principium cognoscendi* of theology is revelation itself (including natural revelation, special revelation, and Christ as revelation).

### Before we move on

+ How do the *principium essendi* and *principium cognoscendi* come to be the same in philosophy?

+ If reason is philosophy's *principium cognoscendi*, what does that mean for the authority of philosophy?

+ What are the *principium essendi* and *principium cognoscendi* of theology? What does this mean for the authority of theology's *principium cognoscendi*?

Now we can broach the question to which all our discussion thus far has been directed: Just what should we think about the relationship of philosophy to theology? What exactly is the role and place of philosophy? In a Reformed context, the answer to that question is straightforward. Reformed theology teaches us that God is the *principium essendi* of *all disciplines*, since it is from God alone that any and every discipline derives anything and everything that it is and has. A simpler way to put this is that God is the Creator and Sustainer of all things (cf. Gen. 1:1ff.; Pss. 104; 139; Eph. 1:11; Heb. 1:3).

Moreover, from a Reformed perspective, the *principium cognoscendi* is the revelation of God, both natural and special. How do we know what we know, about God and about everything else? Not only has God created and sustained all things, but in and through that creation he reveals himself: through what he has made (Ps. 19; Rom. 1:20); through what he says (Heb. 1:1–2); and in and through his Son (Col. 1). Given these foundational and universal truths, theology can be done only because of what God has done, first of all.

But it should be obvious as well that the sweep and scope of theology will be needed for every other discipline that seeks to deal with some aspect of God's creation. Since God's creation includes all things, anything to which a specific discipline is committed will, first and foremost, be something that reveals God, and about which God himself has something to say. If that is the case, then it is the case that every discipline is directly related to the two *principia* of theology. The only way to properly understand God's revelation is through God's own revealed Word, which is the *principium cognoscendi* of theology. Thus, it is theology that ought to set the parameters, the rules, and the laws for the other disciplines. Hendrik Stoker notes:

> The distinction between theology and philosophy does not, according to my opinion, coincide with that between the revelation of God in his Word on the one hand and the cosmos (or created universe) on the other. This is the case, because on the one hand theology also deals with God's revelation in creation, the cosmos, viewed in the light of his Word revelation, whereas the Scriptures on the other hand disclose not only who God is and what his relation to all "things" is, but also matters concerning the created universe (or the cos-

mos) as such. (God's Word even makes assertions on matters relating to the field of some particular science or other, for instance that the laborer [note: not labor] is worthy of his [not of its] reward.) Because to the field of theology belong the ultimate problems, it may be called the "*scientia prima inter pares.*"[5]

### BEFORE WE MOVE ON

+ God is which *principium* for theology, and why?
+ Divine revelation is which *principium* for theology, and why?
+ How do these two *principia* relate to every discipline?
+ What does this mean for the role of theology in any discipline? In philosophy?

The role of philosophy, therefore, must be as subservient to theology. If philosophy seeks to maintain its *principium* of reason, then reason itself must be understood, defined, delineated, and used within the boundaries and context set forth by God and his revelation. To put it negatively, reason does not have the prerogative to act independently of what God has determined. If it does so, it will inevitably end in failure. This takes us back to the illustration above. Reason acting of its own accord is analogous to the man with a map. He does not know where he is, even if he has some idea of where he would like to go. In order to get to where he wants to go, he can only work through a seemingly endless array of "maps," hoping that at some point one map will bring him to his destination. Since he has no idea where he is, he can never argue cogently for his own starting point; he is in the dark.

If, however, reason is properly guided and directed, it is analogous to the man with the GPS. The GPS is a view from above. It tells the man where he is. It shows him how he can move from where he is to make real progress toward his destination. It allows him to choose the proper map. He may have more than one way to move to his desired destination. But he cannot move, even an inch, in the proper direction unless he stays within the map that has been set by the GPS.

In other words, philosophy can be properly pursued only when it is pursued within the context and confines of God's own revelation. Philosophy's role is as a handmaid to theology. Its use is *ministerial*, not *magisterial*. It seeks to serve, not to rule over, theology. It takes its cue from theological truths; it sets its tasks according to principles and ideas that conform to, and are perhaps directed by, God's own Word.

This means, to use just one example, that philosophy has to let the Word of God determine and define *reason's own status*. Since philosophy is (rightly) concerned with principles and uses of reason, it should first consult theology to ascertain just what reason is meant to do and be. When we read, for example, that the mind of man is hostile toward God (Rom. 8:7), and that the natural man cannot understand spiritual things (1 Cor. 2:14), and that we, while remaining in our sins, are dead (Eph. 2:1), we should see that philosophy's tasks cannot begin to be accomplished until and unless reason itself is redeemed in Christ.

### Before we move on

+ How does theology set boundaries and standards for philosophy?

Philosophy that seeks to undertake its task apart from this redemption winds up in foolishness and empty deceit. This is, in part, why the apostle Paul contrasts the sinful pursuit of wisdom (i.e., philosophy apart from Christ) with God's wisdom:

For it is written,

"I will destroy the wisdom of the wise,
　　and the discernment of the discerning I will thwart."

Where is the one who is wise? Where is the scribe? Where is the debater of this age? Has not God made foolish the wisdom of the world? For since, in the wisdom of God, the world did not know God through wisdom, it pleased God through the folly of what we preach to save those who believe. (1 Cor. 1:19–21)

Notice that "the world did not know God through wisdom." Why not? Because the wisdom of the world is in direct opposition to the wisdom of God. The folly of the cross (which is wiser than the wisdom of the world—1 Cor. 1:25) is the beginning of true wisdom. Unless philosophy begins its task with that folly, which is God's wisdom, it will be destroyed; it will destroy itself.

Paul also makes it clear that as the result of the power and presence of sin, for all who are and remain in Adam, the "wisdom" that is pursued is, as a matter of fact, foolishness and is a product of darkened and deceitful hearts (Rom. 1:21ff.). If philosophy seeks to love wisdom and to think that such wisdom can be gained or found apart from Christ, it is foolishness; it is empty and useless. It simply *cannot* fulfill its task. A philosophy that works according to wisdom as defined by the world is vanity and striving after the wind.

Two things should be mentioned here with respect to philosophy's role as subsumed under theology. First, all of what we have said in this regard does not mean, of course, that philosophy has made no contribution to theoretical thinking at all. Much of what philosophy has done, historically, has been useful, and useful to theology. What it does mean is that whatever contribution philosophy has made, when it does, it does so in spite of itself. It does so, we could say, by accident. It does so because it cannot help but do its work in God's world, with God's creation. Given that God does not let man (in Adam) descend to his worst level, there are times when philosophy may have real insight. But a diamond in the rough does not make the rough any more valuable. It is an anomaly; it doesn't belong. It can be mined for what it is, but it can take its place only in its proper context. Second, the role of philosophy as serving theology is anything but the majority opinion. To think of philosophy in this way will not please the guild; it will not bolster the vast majority who have earned their degrees and done their work as if philosophy could get along quite well without God and his revelation to us. That, however, should be of little concern. Let God be true though every man were a liar (Rom. 3:4). The fact that philosophy has made such little (if any) progress ought to be proof enough that something is terribly, even fatally, wrong. But what ought to be does not always determine what is.

BEFORE WE MOVE ON

+ What is the beginning of true wisdom, and why is this problematic for the world?

+ Is it possible for useful insights to be found outside of Christian theology? Why or why not?

## USES AND ABUSES

Once philosophy sets its tasks and goals, which themselves are consistent with theology and which can serve theology, it can thrive and prosper. The Reformed theologian Francis Turretin notes four primary uses of philosophy in theology, once it is established that philosophy's role is as a handmaid to theology, not a mistress. There is, first, a specifically apologetic thrust to the use of philosophy in theology. In this sense, theologians should be quick to use philosophy and its tools, when and where they can, in order to demonstrate something of Christianity's own truth. According to Turretin, this first primary use of philosophy for theology is that

> it serves as a means of convincing the Gentiles and preparing them for the Christian faith. . . . So God wishes us to apply all the truths of the lower sciences to theology and after rescuing them from the Gentiles (as holders of a bad faith) to take and appropriate them to Christ who is the truth, for the building of the mystic temple; as formerly Moses enriched and adorned the tabernacle with the Egyptian gold, and Solomon procured the assistance of the Sidonians and Syrians in building the temple.[6]

An example from Scripture might help to illuminate this point. As Paul waited in Athens for Silas and Timothy, he was moved and provoked because of the conspicuous abundance of idolatry that was present throughout this center of intellectual activity. So he set out to defend the Christian faith, both in the synagogues and in the marketplace. In the course of his defense, some Epicurean and Stoic philosophers became curious (or perhaps agitated) because of Paul's strange teaching that one who had walked the earth had also risen from the dead. This would have been abhorrent to a Greek mind, since the overwhelming consensus of the time was that there was a cyclical pattern to the universe. For one to rise from the dead would mean, rather, that there was a continuity between death and "after death" that would put the lie to a Greek view of history. So they wanted Paul's teaching to be evaluated by the intellectuals in Athens. The Hill of Ares was designed so that just such evaluations could take place. So Paul went before the philosophers, and other Athenians, in order to defend the Christian faith.

Without going into the details of Paul's encounter, a couple of specific passages will help us to understand something of the ministerial use of philosophy for theology. Paul begins his address without attempting to "prove" to the philosophers that the Christian God exists. That is, he was not concerned to set forth syllogisms that would conclude for the existence of the triune God. Rather, Paul begins by telling his audience just what kind of God the Christian God is. Though the philosophers at Athens have concluded that there was some god who could not be known at all, Paul begins by proclaiming to them just what kind of God this is that they think is unknown.

### Before we move on

+ How can apologetics be viewed as a particular service to theology?
+ How does the beginning of Paul's address demonstrate the advantage of the GPS method over the map method? Which *principium* of theology is brought into play?

After this description of God, Paul does something that is quite fascinating, and that points us in a particular direction with respect to our topic. He quotes from two separate Greek philosopher-poets. Why does Paul do this? Is it the case that Paul is quoting from these Greek poets in order to affirm the Greeks in what they had thus far concluded with respect to God? Is Paul attempting simply to add to their otherwise coherent (though incomplete) knowledge of the true God?

It doesn't seem so, and for the following reasons. First, notice Paul's quotes:

For

"In him we live and move and have our being";

as even some of your own poets have said,

"For we are indeed his offspring." (Acts 17:28)[7]

The question we might ask, in the first place, is: Is it true that "in him we live and move and have our being"? That is, is Paul using these quotations because the poets have accurately described the true God, albeit incompletely?

The answer to the first question depends on at least a couple of factors. Without engaging the entire debate concerning propositions, let's agree for our purposes that propositions are bearers of truth-value; they can be either true or false. Let's also agree that propositions are expressed in sentences, such as "In him we live and move and have our being."

In that case, what we have in Paul's quotations are propositions, expressed in sentences, whose meaning depends not simply on the linguistic meaning of the words or sentences themselves, but on the references of the indexical elements of the sentences themselves. For example, when Paul says to those on Mars Hill, "In him we live," to whom is Paul referring? Who is the "him" of "in him"? He is obviously referring to the true God, the God whom he has just described to his listeners, the triune God who "made the world and everything in it," who is "Lord of heaven and earth," who "does not live in temples made by man," who is not "served by human hands, as though he needed anything," who "gives to all mankind life and breath and everything," who "made from one man every nation of mankind to live on all the face of the earth," and who "determined allotted periods and the boundaries of their dwelling place" (Acts 17:24–28). In other words, there was no question to whom Paul was referring when he borrowed the quotations from Epimenides and from Aratus. Given that Paul's reference was to the true God, the propositions are true; they express the truth of the matter as it really is.

Worth noting, however, is that when Epimenides and Aratus wrote these words, the propositions themselves were utterly false. The "him" to which they both refer is not the triune God, but is, rather, a false god (likely Zeus). Thus, the reference of the indexical elements of the propositions as uttered by Paul is the true God, whereas the reference of the indexical elements of the same propositions when uttered by the Greek poets is an idol.

So why does Paul use the very poets who have, in the context of Paul's listeners, promoted not Christianity or true religion, but idolatry? In part, the answer is "persuasion." Paul knew that the reason idolatry existed was not ignorance on the part of the idolaters, but was rather an attempt at complete suppression of the truth as it is found in God's general revelation (Rom. 1:18ff.). So Paul was able to take those statements that were originally idolatrous (pointing to false gods) and transplant them back into their proper biblical context. Thus, he moved them from false and idolatrous expressions to expressions of the truth. In doing that, he took something with which his audience would be familiar and "recontextualized" it, changing its truth-value and its meaning, so that that which was familiar to them became also that which communicated the truth to them, truth that they all knew, but were seeking to suppress. There is value, therefore, in using the language of the philosophers, poets, and others in order to show them just how it is that the truth of Christianity fulfills the aspirations expressed in that language.

### Before we move on

+ What are indexical elements? How do they affect a proposition's truth-value?

+ How did recontextualization allow Paul to turn a false proposition into a true one?

+ How can the language of non-Christians be used to express the truths of Christianity?

Philosophy might also serve theology in a second way: as a "testimony of consent in things known by nature." Here Turretin has in mind the fact that, to the extent that philosophy has its focus in natural revelation, it can be used to better confirm those things that are revealed by God, things that are true and certain in themselves.[8] This is the case because natural and special revelation both reveal God, and together constitute the one truth about him. Perhaps this can be seen, for example, in the way that notions of design present in philosophical discussions today serve to "better confirm" the truth of God's creating and controlling activity.[9]

Third, philosophy can help theology in its ability to properly distinguish and clarify the truth as it is found in Scripture, and in God's revelation generally. "For although reason receives the principles of religion from the light of faith, yet (this light preceding) it ought to judge from these principles how the parts of the heavenly doctrine cohere and mutually establish each other; what is consistent with and what is contrary to them."[10]

Finally, notes Turretin, "the mind may be furnished and prepared by these inferior systems for the reception and management of a higher science." Here another warning is in order. Until and unless one is resolutely grounded in the *principia* of theology, the danger can be almost overwhelming if one goes about the study of philosophy, and perhaps especially philosophy of religion.

Unfortunately, one has to search far and wide for a philosophy of religion that takes seriously its place as a handmaid to theology. Consequently, one need hardly search at all for an article or essay in philosophy or philosophy of religion in which the historic truths of Christianity are not under attack, either implicitly or explicitly. Not only so, but philosophy, because of its subject matter and its general methodology, has an allure to many that is sirenically seductive in its force. So, says Turretin, "this must however be done so carefully that a too great love of philosophy may not captivate us and that we may not regard it as a mistress, but as a handmaid."

### Before we move on

+ Considering the three broad categories of philosophy, how can philosophy help to confirm what is apparent in natural revelation?

+ How can philosophy be useful in clarifying the truth found in Scripture?

+ What is the danger of studying philosophy in order to better study theology?

Turretin goes on to outline the differences in the respective domains of philosophy and theology. Perhaps many of the errors in thinking about the relationship of these two disciplines lie in a failure to grasp the boundaries of each. In that light, four errors are explicitly mentioned by him.

The first error has to do with an illegitimate transfer of principle from philosophy to theology. Specifically, Turretin notes errors maintained, such as that virgins cannot be mothers, in spite of what God's revelation teaches. Though philosophy is correct in its general affirmations, we dare not allow those affirmations to rule out the plain truth of God's Word.

Second, similar to the first error, we must not let false teachings of philosophy be introduced into theology in such a way as to deny Scripture. For example, Aristotle's belief that the world is eternal must not be imported into theology or defended as a theological truth, given that it serves to undermine the teaching of Scripture with regard to creation.

The third error, according to Turretin, is: "When philosophy assumes to itself the office of a master in articles of faith, not content with that of a servant (as was done by the Scholastics who placed Aristotle upon the throne; and by the Socinians who would not admit the doctrines of the Trinity, of the incarnation, etc. because they did not seem to be in accordance with the principles of philosophy)."[11] Turretin mentions this more than once. It may be impossible to overstate the seriousness of this error.

Fourth, Turretin warns against introducing more new phrases or concepts than is necessary into theology "under which . . . new and dangerous errors lie concealed." In order to avoid this error, one must be acutely aware of the concepts, principles, and presuppositions that accompany philosophical language in order either to reconfigure them or to keep from borrowing them altogether.

### Before we close

✠ How does forgetting the *principia* of theology lead to different misuses of philosophy?

Philosophy can find its place and know its role only if it begins with a "GPS," a view from above. It can make progress only if it directs itself according to what God has said. If it will begin there, it has the potential of making unprecedented gains in addressing the serious and important questions that it asks. Those questions can develop, and develop deeply, only when the faith of Reformed theology gives them their reason for being.

### In conclusion

+ Philosophy's task is to make sense out of the world in order to make sense of our place in it. What is theology's task?

+ What are the *principium essendi* and *principium cognoscendi* of philosophy? Where does philosophy begin to answer its questions? Why is this problematic?

+ Why must philosophy serve theology, and how can it best do so?

## GLOSSARY

**Aristotle** (384–322 B.C.). A Greek philosopher who was a student of Plato and the tutor of Alexander the Great. He taught, against Plato, that ultimate reality is found in the particulars of the universe (acts of goodness), rather than in an abstract category (absolute Goodness).

**Enlightenment**. An intellectual movement that prioritized reason and the scientific method over against Scripture as the way to know ultimate reality.

**Epicureanism**. A philosophical school that advocated a worldview in which pleasure was the ultimate good. Living a simple life through restraining one's desires was considered the best way to attain this pleasure.

**Epistemology**. The study of why, how, or whether we know something.

**Erigena, John Scotus** (c. 800–877). An Irish philosopher who modified Plato's philosophy by locating absolute "goodness" in the concept of the Christian God. Later in life, however, he posited that "nature" was the highest principle of being and that it included both God and creation.

**Ethics**. The study of "right" and "wrong." Sometimes *ethics* may refer to the task of determining the rightness or wrongness of a particular action *in itself*. In other cases, *ethics* may refer to the task of determining the obligation (or nonobligation) that a particular situation or circumstance places on a person.

**General Revelation** (or **Natural Revelation**). God's disclosure of himself to man through creation—"the things that have been made" (Rom. 1:20; cf. Ps. 19:1–6)—which is distinct from his direct disclosure (e.g., through speech, theophany, or Scripture).

**Kant, Immanuel** (1724–1804). A German philosopher who attempted to formulate a theory of knowledge that united reason and experience in order to account for the human ability to know reality.

**Laws of Logic**. The rules that govern and structure the human activity of knowing. For example, the law of noncontradiction states, "A cannot be A and *not* A at the same time and in the same way."

**Metaphysics**. The study of ultimate reality—for example, determining the substance of reality, or whether reality is one, two, or many things. Christians understand metaphysics, first and foremost, in terms of the distinction and relation between the Creator and his creation.

**Natural Revelation**. See **General Revelation**.

**Natural Theology**. The task of speaking about God while intentionally neglecting Scripture. This kind of theology is popular in Roman Catholic circles, and philosophy is often used as a substitute for Scripture as one's foundation for speaking about God.

**Philosophy**. A theoretical activity that seeks to make sense out of the world in order to make sense of our place in it.

**Plato** (423–347 B.C.). A Greek philosopher and tutor of Aristotle who taught that ultimate reality is found in an ethereal realm of forms (absolute Goodness) and not in earthly manifestations of those forms (acts of goodness).

**Pre-Socratic**. The three major philosophers of the Greek world were Socrates, his student Plato, and Plato's student Aristotle. Pre-Socratic philosophers were those theorists who investigated the nature and foundation of the external world (metaphysics) before Socrates (fifth century B.C. and earlier).

*Principium* (plural: *principia*). The basic, fundamental, and necessary truths that provide for the existence and coherence of a particular discipline.

*Principium Cognoscendi*. The source or ground of the knowledge of something.

*Principium Essendi*. The source or ground of the existence of something.

**Reason**. The ability to apply the laws of logic to the task of acquiring knowledge. Sometimes *reason* is used to refer to the laws of logic themselves.

**Revelation**. God's disclosure of himself to man.

**Scholastics**. A school of medieval philosophers (of whom Thomas Aquinas is the most famous) who prized argumentative forms of reasoning in order to defend Christian dogma. Ultimately, however, many scholastics incorporated much of Aristotle's secular philosophy into their Christian doctrines in order to defend them.

**Socinianism**. A form of Christian heresy that prioritized various philosophical principles over against Scripture's teaching on key Christian doctrines such as the Trinity, the incarnation, the efficacy of the atonement, and original sin.

**Socrates** (496–399 B.C.). A Greek philosopher and tutor of Plato whose writings have had a significant impact on the realm of ethics.

**Special Revelation**. God's disclosure of himself to man through his acts, presence, or direct speech. It is only through special revelation that man may attain saving knowledge of what God has done in Christ (John 1:17–18; 14:6–21; Heb. 1:3).

**Stoicism**. A school of Greek philosophy that taught that one must overcome and eradicate emotions, which are destructive, through intellectual and moral focus.

**Tillich, Paul** (1886–1965). A German philosopher and liberal theologian who is best known for attempting to use Christian theology to answer questions of secular philosophy, particularly in the area of human experience and existence.

## NOTES

1. Peter van Inwagen, *Metaphysics*, 2nd ed. (Boulder, CO: Westview Press, 2002), 12. Even with respect to "their assertions," van Inwagen notes that the best that can be done is to get the actual words right, and then pick the best argument as to the interpretation of those words.

2. See K. Scott Oliphint, *God With Us: Divine Condescension and the Attributes of God*, (Wheaton, IL: Crossway Books, 2012).

3. See Herman Dooyeweerd, *A New Critique of Theoretical Thought*, trans. David H. Freeman and William S. Young, 4 vols. (Nutley, NJ: Presbyterian and Reformed, 1969).

4. In the interest of space and clarity, we will continue to use the Latin term *principia* in order to highlight the complexity of its meaning. We will use it to denote the principle, source, ground, and justification of something.

5. That is, "the first science among equals." Hendrik G. Stoker, "Reconnoitering the Theory of Knowledge of Professor Dr. Cornelius Van Til," in *Jerusalem and Athens: Critical Discussions on the Philosophy and Apologetics of Cornelius Van Til*, ed. E. R. Geehan (Nutley, NJ: Presbyterian and Reformed, 1977), 39.

6. Francis Turretin, *Institutes of Elenctic Theology*, ed. James T. Dennison Jr., trans. George Musgrave Giger, 3 vols. (Phillipsburg, NJ: P&R Publishing, 1994–97), 1.45f. All four points will be taken from this source.

7. The first quotation is likely from Epimenides of Crete, the latter from Aratus's poem "Phainomena."

8. The central truths of theology, according to Turretin, "are founded upon certain and indubitable principles and truths known per se." It is not the case, therefore, that there is a necessary connection between philosophy's task and theology's task. Rather, philosophy, given its subservient status, may help to clarify what is otherwise known. Turretin, *Institutes*, 1.47.

9. This "confirmation" does not address the stickier problem of the use of design arguments for apologetic purposes. Those arguments can, of course, be used, just so long as one's approach neither sacrifices nor undermines the *principia* of theology—that is, just so long as one's *principium cognoscendi* (Scripture), as grounded in the *principium essendi* (the triune God), is not compromised in the method used to set forth such arguments.

10. Turretin, *Institutes*, 1.45.

11. Ibid., 1.46.